Ancient Greek Homes

Haydn Middleton

Heinemann Library
Chicago, Illinois

© 2003 Reed Educational & Professional Publishing
Published by Heinemann Library,
an imprint of Reed Educational & Professional Publishing,
Chicago, Illinois
Customer Service 888-454-2279
Visit our website at www.heinemannlibrary.com

Text and cover designed by Tinstar
Illustrations by Jeff Edwards, Art Construction, and Martin Smillie
Originated by Ambassador Litho
Printed by Wing King Tong in Hong Kong

07 06 05 04 03
10 9 8 7 6 5 4 3 2 1

Library of Congress Cataloging-in-Publication Data
Middleton, Haydn.
  Ancient Greek Homes / Haydn Middleton.
    p. cm. -- (People in the past)
  Includes bibliographical references and index.
  ISBN 1-58810-636-5 (HC) 1-4034-0132-2 (Pbk)
    1. Dwellings--Greece--History--To 1500--Juvenile literature. 2.
Family--Greece--History--To 1500--Juvenile literature. [1.
Dwellings--Greece--History. 2. Greece--Civilization--To 146 B.C.]   I.
Title. II. Series.
  DF99 .M54 2002
  938--dc21
                            2001005214

Acknowledgments
The publisher would like to thank the following for permission to reproduce photographs:
Ancient Art and Architecture Collection, pp. 6, 7, 11, 24, 27, 32, 39, 40; CM Dixon, pp. 8, 35; Michael Holford, pp. 10, 38; Corbis, pp. 12, 21, 34; AKG London, pp. 13, 14, 22, 26, 28, 31, 36, 37; British Museum, p. 18; Ashmolean Museum, p. 30.

Cover photograph reproduced with permission of AKG/Erich Lessing

Some words are shown in bold, **like this.** You can find out what they mean by looking in the glossary.

Contents

The World of the Ancient Greeks

When people talk about ancient Greece, they do not just mean the modern-day country of Greece as it used to be. The ancient Greek world was made up of the hot, rocky mainland of Greece and hundreds of islands in the Aegean, Ionian, and Adriatic Seas, as well as further settlements overseas, in places ranging from northern Africa to what we now call Turkey and Italy. The earliest Greek speakers did not think that they all belonged to a single country. For a long time, they did not even think that they all belonged to the same **civilization.**

For centuries, the mightiest people in the Greek world were the Minoans, based on the island of Crete. Power then passed to the warlike Mycenaeans, based on the mainland, in the region known as the **Peloponnese.** This was followed, around 1100 B.C.E., by centuries of confusion and upheaval.

Later, in the Classical Age, from about 500 B.C.E. until about 300 B.C.E., prosperity was restored by the rise of many city-states, such as Athens and Sparta. The Greek word for city-state is *polis.* Each *polis* was a large city that controlled the villages and farmland around it.

Vanishing houses

Daily life varied from place to place in the ancient Greek world, and the homes in which people lived probably varied as well. Very few houses from that time have survived. We can still see many ruins of large Greek temples and other public buildings because these were built to last, from stone and marble. Most private houses, on the other hand, were made of less permanent materials such as sunbaked mud bricks. Even if a larger house had floors of stone, people would often take away the stone after the house was left empty, to use on other buildings. Very few homes from that time exist for **archaeologists** to examine today.

However, from ancient books, as well as from archaeological remains, there is enough evidence to piece together what Greek homes were like. This evidence also gives us a glimpse of what life was like for the men, women, and children who lived in them more than 2,000 years ago.

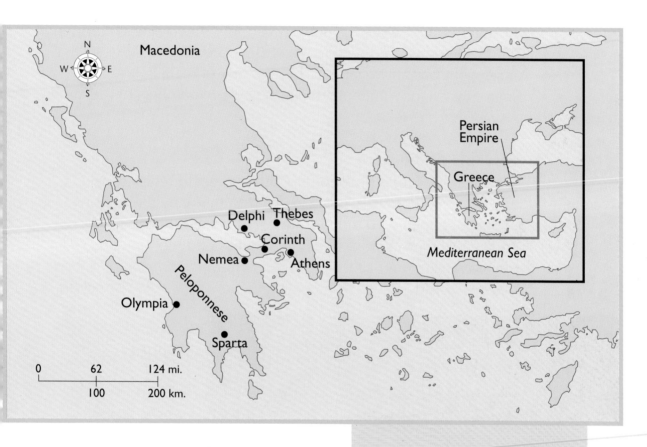

Ancient Greece was not a single, unified country but was instead a collection of many separate states that varied greatly in size and strength. The ancient Greeks used the word *Hellas* to describe all the places where there was a Greek way of life.

The Family

Ancient Greek life was largely run by men and for the benefit of men. The ancient Greek men held all the public jobs and had many more legal rights than did the women. The basic unit of Greek society, from the richest to the poorest, was the family. In the homes of some families, three generations lived under a single roof: grandparents, a married son and his wife, and their children. In larger homes, there might even be more relatives, such as those who were unmarried, widowed, or divorced. The head of such a household was always a man, but the task of making it run smoothly fell to women, whether they were members of the family, servants, or slaves.

Servants of the state

"It is a crime," the **philosopher** Plato wrote, "to refuse to take a wife." Greek men were fully expected to marry by the age of 35. In Sparta, a man who did not marry could have all his rights as a **citizen** taken away from him. The families of the bride and groom often arranged marriages that were **economic** unions, rather than matches based on love. By merging the fortunes of two families, more wealth could be created for the *polis.*

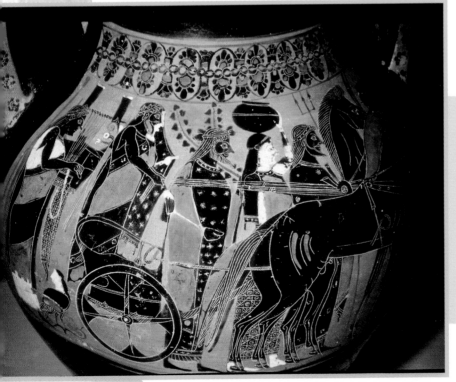

This vase shows a bride and groom walking in their wedding procession. Brides brought gifts called **dowries** to their new husbands. A wealthy girl's dowry could be as much as ten percent of her father's wealth or property.

This vase shows a Greek woman serving a man some food. Greek women had far fewer rights than most women do today. They were seldom supposed to leave the home, let alone get jobs or have a say in the way that the *polis* was governed.

It was important for people to marry so that they could have children. Children made sure that the *polis* would stay strong over time. Sons would one day fight to protect the state in wars, and daughters would give birth to future heads of the household. All children would eventually care for their elderly parents.

Even city-states as large as Athens had no regular police forces. For that reason, governments relied heavily on the heads of each family to make sure that all the members of their households, as well as any servants and slaves, obeyed the law. In that way, individual households were like miniature city-states, with their own rulers.

The Spartan exception

The family unit in Sparta was organized on unusual lines. There, the state government, not heads of families, laid down strict rules for everyone. Boys were sent away from home at the age of seven years, to live together in army **barracks** and to train to be full-time soldiers. After the age of 30, they might take wives and live in normal homes. Even then, they were often away on military campaigns for months on end. This meant that Spartan women had more independence in the management of their households. Unlike women elsewhere in Greece, they could even own a home, and could make decisions about what to do with it.

The *Oikos*

The Greek word for a house was *oikos*. This word was used for the materials used to make the house, such as bricks. The word *oikos* also meant the house itself, and it was used to refer to the family that lived inside it, that is, the household. It could also mean a wealthy family's **estate.**

Family fortunes

In Athens, the estates did not pass as a whole from father to son. They were often split apart, on the owner's death, among his surviving **heirs.** Great fortunes could be made or lost quickly, depending on how careful the new owners were with the money.

The figure seated here is Zeus, the head of household of Greek gods and goddesses, who lived on Mount Olympus.

The **philosopher** Plato wrote a book called *The Republic,* about how a **polis** should be run. Plato wrote about the importance of being careful with family money. In the book, a wealthy man says, "As a money-maker I hold a place somewhere between my grandfather and my father. For my grandfather … inherited about as much as I now possess and multiplied it many times, my father Lysanias reduced it below the present amount, and I'll be happy if I leave to these boys a little more and no less than I inherited."

An *oikos* could be ruined if the head of the household lost family money through gambling, horse breeding, or domestic entertainment. In the 420s B.C.E., a man called Kallias inherited so much money that he was thought to be the richest man in Greece. Within 40 years, his extravagance had helped to reduce the worth of the family property from more than 1,200,000 **drachmas** to less than 12,000 *drachmas*. By comparison, many who did hard, physical work earned just one *drachma* a day.

Over the course of five generations, only one family in Classical Athens was always in the wealthiest class. Meanwhile, 357 other families seemed to pass from poor to rich and back to poor in just one generation. It is important to remember what an unstable world the ancient Greeks lived in, as we look at the kinds of homes in which they lived.

Human Tools

Historians used to believe that most Athenian households had at least one domestic slave. However, slaves would have been expensive to buy and also to provide food for, so they may not have been quite so common. Even so, in 5th-century-B.C.E. Athens, there were between 80,000 and 100,000 slaves. That was one slave for every free member of the population. Most of them were foreigners, such as **Persians** captured during warfare, and others were the children of slaves.

Slaves in Sparta, Thessaly, or Sicily often led hard lives, but Athenian slaves could sometimes be mistaken for regular members of a family. It made sense for families to treat their slaves with some

consideration. The writer Aristotle described them as "human tools," and it did not make sense for a person to mistreat his own tools. Some slaves could eventually buy their own freedom and go on—as did the banker Pasion, a former slave—to become highly successful businessmen.

This bronze statue shows an African who was captured and made to serve as a slave in ancient Greece.

Slaves in the home

Greek authors wrote about household slaves who had various specific tasks: female slaves assisted with child care, while male slaves worked in the kitchen or answered the door to visitors. The behavior of

On this vase, women are shown drawing water from a well. Female slaves were seen in public more often than rich women. They might also be sent outside the home to work as cooks, cleaners, nannies, or grape pickers.

slaves was not always very **servile.** In the book *Protagoras,* by the **philosopher** Plato, a bad-tempered slave at the house of Kallias slams the door in the face of the philosopher Socrates. It is probable that masters punished their slaves by beating and even torturing them. Yet some close relationships were formed. According to the Athenian writer Xenophon's *Memoirs of Socrates,* men were more likely to grieve over a slave's death than to grieve over the death of a friend.

Evidence suggests that slaves did not have their own separate **quarters** in either town or country houses. Xenophon mentioned a house in which the male slaves slept in the *andron,* or men's part of the house, and female slaves in the *gunaikon,* or women's part of the house. Since slaves lived so intimately with their masters, it is easy to understand why a character in Euripides' play *Helen* says, "It is bad not to feel with your masters, laugh with them, and sympathize in their sorrows."

Building Materials

Public buildings in ancient Greece , such as temples, theaters, and law courts, were built with stone so they would last. The ruins of many public buildings can still be seen today, more than 2,000 years later. However, the ancient Greeks, unlike the Romans of later centuries, were less interested in building large, elaborate homes for themselves. This was partly because the hot, dry Greek climate made it possible to spend a great deal of time outdoors.

In both the city and the country, most ordinary houses built between 500 and 300 B.C.E. were made of sunbaked mud bricks over a stone foundation. They had dirt floors, roofs covered in thatch or tiles made of clay, and small windows with wooden shutters but no glass. These structures were much less permanent than the public buildings were. Burglars were known as wall piercers. If walls could be pierced, then they cannot have been very solid.

There is even less evidence of basic Greek home furnishings. Wooden chests, couches, chairs, stools, and tables tend to decay over the centuries, so we must examine ancient images to see how they might once have looked. Fortunately, some floors made of pebble **mosaic** have been found.

This image of a seated woman opening a box is from the 5th century B.C.E. The interior furnishings look fancy, but most homes probably had little external decoration.

Piecing the past together

Houses have been **excavated** on sites all over the Greek world. In cities they seem to have been packed closely together in blocks. Most of the walls and roofs have long since vanished—leaving only the base of the stone foundations. From these, it is often hard to tell even where the entrances to different rooms might have been. **Archaeologists** have figured out that some houses had an upper story, after finding stone bases that would once have supported wooden staircases.

At house sites, archaeologists often find pottery fragments, objects made from stone or metal, and coins. If pieces of plates are found in a certain area, then that might mean that once it was a dining room, or it might simply mean that this was the part of the house where broken dishes were dumped.

The coming of concrete

Southern Italy and Sicily were part of the **Hellenistic** world. From Italy, in the late 3rd century B.C.E., came a new building technique, construction in concrete. In time, concrete became the best material for the construction of **vaults** in more elaborate buildings. It was cheap, strong, water resistant, and fireproof, and it could easily be used on big projects by unskilled workers, who were sometimes slaves or prisoners of war. In some cities, the ancient Greeks used concrete to build homes that were a lot like high-rise apartment buildings.

This picture of a young woman admiring herself in a hand mirror comes from a vase painting from about 430 B.C.E. An open door behind her shows a bedroom.

Different Kinds of Homes

Family houses were often built from similar materials, but they differed depending on which part of the Greek—or **Hellenistic**—world they were built in and when they were built. They also differed depending on how much money was spent on them and on the personal tastes of their owners. From writings and archaeological remains, we have more evidence of larger, more lavish homes than of smaller ones, which were usually made of materials that broke down over time and disappeared easily.

Many Greek houses did have common features. In the 5th–3rd centuries B.C.E., most houses were built around an open courtyard with a **portico** along at least one side. Many household jobs were done in this courtyard, which might contain a well. A number of rooms would lead off it, and visitors were entertained in these rooms. One room might be a small store, with its own street entrance. Other rooms might be bedrooms and storerooms. Writers mentioned houses that had their own gymnasiums and bathrooms, but these must have been unusual.

The courtyard of the House of the Dionysus on Delos was built in the late 2nd century B.C.E. A large tank beneath it stored the house's water supply.

Hellenistic houses

From Hellenistic times, we have evidence of expensive new homes that were built for wealthy officials and merchants and their families. These high-quality houses in cities such as Priene and Delos usually were focused around a small courtyard. They had at least one big reception room that often opened off the north side of a **peristyle,** so that it could catch the sunlight in winter. The surfaces inside were protected and made attractive by mosaic pavements and painted **stucco** wall decorations. There might also have been statues or marble furniture set in the **colonnades.**

courtyard

colonnades

peristyle

0   16   32 ft.
  5   10 m.

This is a drawing of what a peristyle house in Delos would have looked like.

Large houses

Some Greek houses were far bigger than others. Kallias was one of the richest men in Athens. The courtyard of his home had two colonnades around it, each of which was so wide that a number of men were able to walk side by side within it. We know that from this description in Plato's *Protagoras*: "When we entered the house, we found Protagoras walking about in the portico, and walking around with him in a line were on one side Kallias, son of Hipponikos and his half-brother Paralos, the son of Pericles, and Charmides, the son of Glaukon; on the other side were Pericles' other son, Xanthippos and Philippides, son of Philomelos, and Antimoiros of Mende."

Homes in the City

In modern Greece, many towns and cities now stand on the sites of ancient cities. This makes it hard for **archaeologists** to gain access to the remains of older buildings. Sometimes there are no remains at all, since durable materials, such as stone, have been reused in later buildings. As a result, we cannot be sure how most Greek cities were laid out or what the homes in them were like.

However, in 1928, archaeological work began at a site on the Chalkidiki Peninsula, in northern Greece. There, 3,000 years ago, the city of Olynthos was settled. Olynthos had residential areas that, by the end of the 5th century B.C.E., spread over two flat-topped hills. The politician Demosthenes recorded that, in 348 B.C.E., the army of Philip II of Macedon destroyed the city and enslaved any surviving inhabitants. No one ever lived on the site again, so the archaeologists who excavated at Olynthos were given a rare glimpse of exactly how an ancient city was laid out. They explored more than 100 houses from 1928 until 1938, and what they found is a vital source of information on Greek homes.

Archaeologists and historians use imagination and experience to work out what ancient Greek houses might once have looked like. This is a suggestion of how one of the larger houses at Olynthos might have looked.

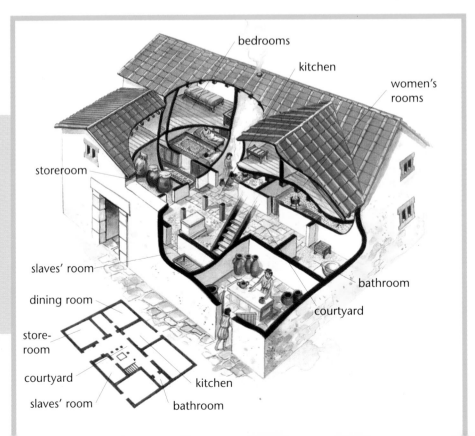

bedrooms

kitchen

women's rooms

storeroom

slaves' room

dining room

store-room

courtyard

slaves' room

bathroom

courtyard

kitchen

bathroom

City blocks

Many of the houses at Olynthos formed city blocks of a standard size. Each block consisted of two rows of houses, with each row sharing **party walls.** Each row had enough space for five houses measuring roughly 56 feet x 56 feet (17 meters x 17 meters), or about 1,041 square feet (289 square meters) in all.

The two rows of houses were separated by a *stenopos*, a narrow alley for drainage. The mud-brick walls and the tiled roofs had almost entirely disappeared, so it was hard for the archaeologists to tell if the houses had one or two stories. Most of the homes had just one entrance, at the front, but next to the front door some had a double door that was used by carts delivering supplies or items of furniture. The delivery doors were normally on north or south side of the house.

Seen from above, a standard city block at Olynthos would have looked like this plan.

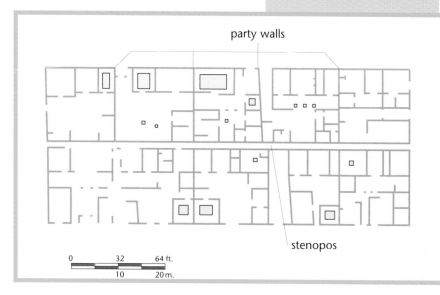

party walls

stenopos

0   32   64 ft.

10   20 m.

Homes of the Rich

From archaeological remains, it is not always easy to tell which ancient houses belonged to rich people. It would seem likely for richer families to have lived in bigger homes, but as the politician Demosthenes pointed out, the houses of Athens' leading government officials used to look very similar to those of poorer citizens. Some houses, such as that of the wealthy Kallias, were larger than others. If a house had a bathroom, or plaster on its walls and mosaics on its floors, it probably belonged to a well-off family. With many slaves and servants in the household, however, the owners still might not have had much space to themselves.

This painting from a vase shows Greek women, probably from wealthy backgrounds, holding domestic utensils. Note the elegant chair that can just be made out on the right of the painting.

A lack of luxury goods

Another way for **archaeologists** to tell if rich people lived in a particular house is by examining the objects found on the site. Again, one would expect rich people to have left behind some precious personal items. Unfortunately, wooden articles could have rotted away over time, and although metal goods are less perishable, they may have been taken away long ago because of their value.

Interestingly, it seems that Greek people did not share our modern desire to spend money on **consumer durables.** "When someone has enough furniture for his house," wrote Xenophon, "he stops buying it there and then." He added that no man had ever had so much silver that he did not want more of it. This suggests that the Greeks were interested in showing off their wealth with expensive **status symbols.** They had no need for expensive labor-saving devices, since they had slaves to do all the time-consuming chores.

Paintings show us the sparse way in which rich people usually furnished and decorated their homes. The teacher and writer Theophrastus made fun of a greedy, ambitious man for having not only a luxurious house but also a pet monkey, a short-tailed ape, Sicilian doves, Laconian dogs, dice made from gazelle horn, walking sticks from Sparta, and a **Persian** carpet. Obviously, this was not typical, but we know very little about the luxury items owned by other wealthy Athenians.

Modest belongings

In 415 B.C.E., about 50 Athenians, most of whom were wealthy, were found to be guilty of vandalizing statues. As punishment, their goods were all sold in an auction, and **inscriptions** survive that record the details of the sale. There we can read how much land and how many valuable homes and slaves the guilty men owned. Yet their personal goods amounted to little more than a pile of bronze pots, kitchen utensils, and clothes. Their cash and items made from precious metals went straight into the treasury of the city-state.

Homes in the Country

In ancient Greek documents, the words *aulion* and *epaulis* were used to describe houses outside the cities. What these words meant varied widely from place to place. They sometimes meant a country farmhouse or even a kind of palace. At other times, they meant just an animal shelter. You might think that country farmhouses would be very different from **urban** dwellings. Homes in the country and the city both seem to have been built along much the same lines, possibly because most households depended on agricultural produce for their survival. For this reason, a similar range of facilities, such as storerooms, would have been required.

Moving away

Nowadays when people move out of a house, they usually leave behind things like doors, lights, and shutters. This does not seem to have been so in ancient Greece. The historian Thucydides wrote that when people fled from the countryside around Athens during the **Peloponnesian** War, they took these things with them. Other documents show that houses were rented out sometimes without doors. When houses were sold, doors were listed as part of the furniture and therefore were not part of the sale. By taking your door with you, you could make your next house look familiar and comforting right away.

One house **excavated** at Vari was laid out like this. On the next page, you can find out what each of the numbered inner spaces might have been used for.

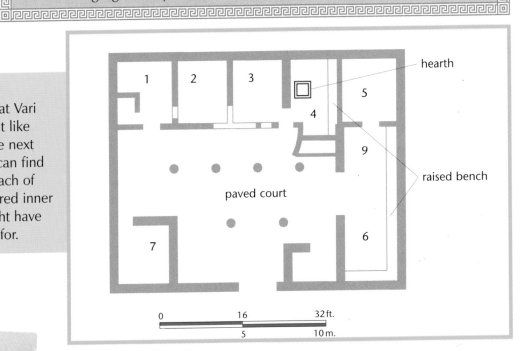

Evidence from Vari

Excavations at Vari, in Attica, have given us a good idea of what a big country house looked like toward the end of the 4th century B.C.E..

The house diagrammed in the picture on page 20 was about 43 feet by 59 feet (about 13 meters by 18 meters) large, and included a large paved courtyard at the building's center and south. The house's single entrance led directly into this courtyard, while a **portico** probably once sheltered the entrances to the rooms on its north and east sides. In room 1, there were traces of burning, so a cooking hearth or **brazier** may have been located here. In room 4, there was another hearth for cooking. Also in room 4, as well as rooms 6 and 9, which run into each other, a stone bench along the wall may have been used as a base for seats or couches.

The most secluded and most private part in the house seems to have been room 5. The **archaeologists** found no evidence to suggest what went on in this room. It may have had no special function at all. In city and country houses alike, rooms often served a variety of different purposes for different members of the household. Finally, room 7 was built on very solid foundations, perhaps because it was the base of a two-story tower, or *pyrgos*. We know that country houses elsewhere sometimes had such towers. Perhaps they were used as lookouts in times of war. Parts of these towers have remained, although the houses that they once belonged to have disappeared.

Homes of the Poor

It can be hard to decide if a house that has been **excavated** once belonged to a poor family. According to ancient Greek writers, several poor families might all live under the same roof, but archaeological remains cannot tell us how many people lived in any house. Since the dwellings of the very poorest people were probably made of cheap materials, it is also unlikely that they would have survived.

Poor households at Olynthos?

The archaeologists at Olynthos, in northern Greece, found a range of homes. Some of them were very small, with no traces of decoration, and they had very little privacy. Just inside their front doors, it would have been possible to look into the entire interior. This made it hard to separate women's **quarters** and men's

The worker at the plow that these oxen pull would have lived in a small home.

quarters, unless curtains or wooden partitions were used to mark off spaces inside. Because the rooms were so small already, this might not have been practical. Fabric or wood would have rotted away, so we cannot tell if curtains or partitions were used.

It is probable that such homes belonged to people of low **status.** Few or no slaves would have lived there, and the female residents would not have needed separate quarters because they spent much of their time doing **menial** jobs outside the home to supplement the family income. Poor women might work in the fields or as servants or nurses. They enjoyed more freedom than did wealthier women, even though they were not considered to be as respectable.

Bigger, more elaborate homes are more interesting to **archaeologists** because they often contained wall paintings, mosaics, or beautiful decorated pottery. Many bigger homes have been excavated, so it is tempting to believe that these were typical ancient Greek homes. However, homes that really were more typical—of a far rougher and simpler sort—are almost invisible to us today because they were not built to last.

Plato on the poor

According to the **philosopher** Plato, every Greek *polis* was in fact two separate *poleis*: one was made up of the rich, and the other was made up of the poor. Each had its own way of life and its own values, and each did not get along with the other. There was a clear physical difference between men of different status too. Poor men were often thin and sunburned from having to work so hard outdoors in the hot Greek climate. Most rich men were pale and flabby. Plato believed that, if poor men in a time of war found themselves fighting alongside the rich, then they would despise them and demand equality.

Organizing the Home

Like the woman painted on this vase, wealthy women spent much of their time organizing the household and supervising slaves in their daily duties.

"'Did you teach your wife everything which relates to the management of a house?' asked Socrates.

"'I did,' replied Ischomachus, 'but not before I had implored the assistance of the gods, to show me what instructions were necessary for her.'"

Suitable homes

Xenophon wrote the paragraphs above, describing the different roles that men and women played in the ancient Greek household. Ischomachus, a man of some wealth, went on to describe what he taught his wife. The following is what he said about the layout of his house, which helps to fill in the picture that we have begun to draw from the discoveries of **archaeologists**:

"She first learned what a house was properly designed for; that it was not ordained to be filled with curious paintings or carvings, or such unnecessary decorations; but that the house should be built with due consideration, and for the convenience of its inhabitants.… The most private and strongest room in the house seems to demand that money, jewels and other things that are rich and valuable should be placed there; the dry places expect corn; the cooler parts are most convenient for the wine; and the more **lightsome** and airy parts of the house for such things as require such a situation.

"I showed her which were the most convenient places for parlors and dining-rooms, that they might be cool in summer and warm in winter; and also, that as the front of the house stood to the south, it had the advantage of the winter's sun, and in the summer it rejoiced more in the shade. Then I appointed the bedrooms, and the nursery, and apartments for the women, divided from the men's lodging." On the next page, you can read more about this division of the home between men and women.

The house as a hive

Ischomachus bossed his wife around, but as mistress of the household, he said, she was like a queen bee: "She stays always in the hive, taking care that all the bees … are working; and those whose business lies outside the home, she sends out to do their duties. These bees, when they bring home their burdens, she receives, and instructs them to store their harvest till the time comes to use it. Then she shares it out fairly among those of her colony. She employs the bees who stay at home in **disposing** and ordering the [honey] combs … and likewise takes care of the young bees, seeing that they are well nourished and educated until they are able to go out and work for their living." The "young bees" of a Greek home would have been children and possibly other relatives.

The Zone of Hestia

The Greek way of looking at the world was different from ours. They tended to see everything as divided into opposites: Greeks and **barbarians, citizens** and *metics,* free men and slaves, and males and females. To their minds, no bridges could be built between these opposites. They were too different.

There were also different areas, or zones, within the *polis,* which were watched over by particular **deities.** In cities, there were two very carefully defined zones. One zone was that of Hestia, the goddess of hearth and home, and the other was that of Hermes, the god of the threshold and the paths which led away from it. In other words, there was an indoor "female" zone and an outdoor "male" zone. While men went out of the home to work, women were supposed to stay at home as the "trusty guardians of what's inside," according to the Athenian writer Apollodorus.

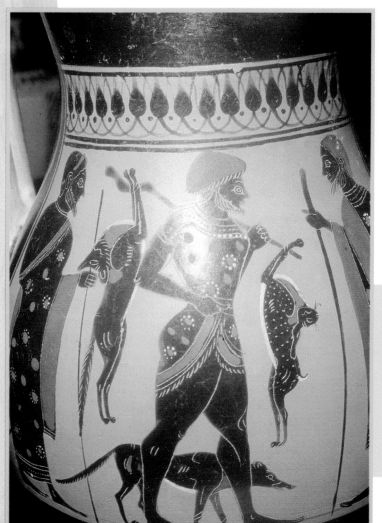

An ancient Greek man is shown bringing home meat. While women stayed at home, in the zone of Hestia, the men went out to work and to hunt, so that they could provide for their families.

Gunaikon and andron

Historians now argue over just how housebound most women were. It does seem that richer women, at least, were seldom seen in public. They were expected to supervise the running of their households, to make clothing, and to raise the children—all under their own roofs.

There could even be opposed areas within the home itself. The male area was known as the *andron* and the female area was known as the *gunaikon*. Since women spent more time in the home than men did, the *gunaikon* was usually the larger of these areas. The female zone included the parts of the house in which they cooked, did their weaving and spinning, looked after children, and sometimes even slept.

This image, on a vase from the 4th century B.C.E., shows a seated woman attended by a maid who would have helped to run her household.

Hestia

Hestia was an important goddess. According to the ancient Greek myths, she was the older sister of Zeus, the king of the gods. When she was young, two gods were fighting over which of them would marry her. Hestia did not want fighting among the gods, so she told Zeus that she would never marry. Zeus rewarded her by making her the goddess of the household. Unlike the other gods and goddesses, Hestia did not leave Mount Olympus to interfere with humans. Instead, she stayed home to care for the fire and run the household. Hestia was honored by the ancient Greeks as the kindest of all the gods. The Greeks associated her with security, happiness, and hospitality.

The *Andron*

◄►

In Classical Athens, women seem to have kept to a house's more private rooms while the men used its public spaces. In larger homes, women's **quarters** were located far away from the street entrance, which was guarded by a male slave. In smaller homes, women might work and relax on an upper story. We do not know how strictly separated men and women were, or for how much of the time.

This vase painting shows Greek men reclining on their couches at a party in the *andron*. The guests ate with knives, spoons, and fingers. Entertainment is being provided by the musician, who is standing.

From the 5th century B.C.E., Greek writers mentioned that one room in the *andron* was elaborately decorated. When **archaeologists** examine an ancient Greek home, this room is easy to identify.

The showpiece room

The *andron* was a small, almost square space. Its doorway was off center, to allow long couches to be placed along the wall next to it. This was the room in which men gave banquets or parties. Often, since it was a place for guests, the *andron* was close to the main entrance, so it might therefore have windows opening onto the street. When it was not being used for entertainment, it is possible that the whole family used it too.

Some *androns* have been found with floors of pebble **mosaic.** According to writers, some were decorated with **frescoes** and tapestries or with big pieces of pottery that were hung from the walls. There might also be round pictures called *tondos.* These showed funny or shocking scenes and were kept turned to the wall, for a guest to take a peek at if he was curious.

The *Symposium*

In Classical times (from about 500 to 300 B.C.E.), the best-known activity that took place in the *andron* was an all-male party called a *symposium*. A great deal of fine Greek poetry, music, and pottery was created for these events, which took a similar form all over the Greek world. Nowadays a "symposium" means a gathering, usually of highly educated people (male and female alike), to discuss matters of common interest. In ancient Greece it was sometimes more of a party.

At the *Symposium*

Since there might be as few as three couches in the *andron*—though usually there were 7—the groups could be quite small. In the room stood a large mixing bowl, or *krater*, in which wine was mixed with water and then was poured by young male or female slaves into fine cups. Poetry and music were performed, and the men would speak in turn on a chosen theme.

Plato's *symposium*

Sometimes at a *symposium* the guests would entertain each other by singing along to a **lyre,** telling jokes and riddles, reciting verses, or having serious discussions about important topics. The **philosopher** Plato wrote an account of one such discussion. In this account, called *The Symposium,* brilliant Athenians debated about what they thought love meant. The modern meaning of the word "symposium" comes from this piece of writing.

This young man is carrying a couch to be used at a *symposium*.

Why was the *symposium* important?

Hosting a *symposium* was a way for an ancient Greek man to show off his home, his wealth, and his importance within the *polis*. A *symposium* was an opportunity for the man of the house to talk with neighbors or friends about things that were going on with the government of the *polis*. He could hold a *symposium* to encourage his guests to vote with him on a certain issue. These meetings were not always about politics, though. Sometimes the ancient Greeks would host a *symposium* for the same reason people host parties now—to enjoy spending time with their friends.

In this scene (from c. 460 B.C.E.) showing an all-male *symposium*, the standing figure is a young cupbearer, trained to mix and serve the wine that was drunk during the evening.

Good manners

In his play, *Wasps*, Aristophanes showed two men having this discussion: "Come and lie down, and learn how to behave at *symposia* and parties." "How do I do it, then? Come on, tell me." "Elegantly." "You mean like this?" "Oh, *no*." "How then?" "Straighten your knees and pour yourself over the cushions, flowing like an athlete. Then praise one of the statues, inspect the ceiling, admire the hangings in the hall."

Kitchen Quarters

Although men might go to market to buy or order fresh food, women had the job of cooking it. When the sites of ancient homes are **excavated,** it is sometimes hard to tell exactly where the kitchen was. If pieces of bone, along with deposits of ash, are found in certain parts of the flooring, then this may mean that a kitchen and its oven once stood on that spot. If pieces of bathroom pottery are found there too, then that may mean that the same indoor fire was used both for cooking and for heating bathwater.

This ancient Greek statue shows a woman cooking a meal. Greek foods were believed to have certain powers over the body: moistening, drying, or heating. A good cook was expected to combine these powers successfully.

In the homes of the rich, most kitchen work was done by female slaves. That gave their mistresses time to dream up exciting menus. The first cookbooks came from ancient Greece, and fragments from them show how popular fish dishes were. "Cut off the head of the ribbon fish," said one of the earliest surviving published recipes. "Wash it and cut it into slices. Pour cheese and oil over it."

Opson and *sitos*

Many Classical Greeks probably ate just one meal a day. This was the evening meal, or *deipnon*. This did not consist of the two main elements of nourishment, food and drink, that we have today. The ancient Greeks had three such elements. They had drinks, usually either wine diluted by water or just water, which were taken after the food. Their food was divided into two elements: the *sitos*, or **staple,** which was usually bread made at home from grain, and the *opson*, which was what was eaten on the *sitos*. The *opson* could be almost anything else, including olives, onions, garlic, and fish. Meat was uncommon except at feast times, when animals were sacrificed, cooked, and eaten.

Different drinking practices

The Greeks were proud to be wine drinkers. To them, only **barbarians** drank beer. In its raw form, Greek wine was sweet and strong and usually had grape and vine debris floating in it. It had to be sieved before it was mixed with water and poured. The Classical Athenians liked to drink socially in "rounds" at their *symposia*, passing cups around, with one toast after another. Spartans were more solitary drinkers, with each man drinking from his own cup. This cup, called a *kothon*, could easily be carried in a soldier's knapsack. It had ridges to hold back any impurities in the water that Spartans had to drink when they were on the march.

Bathrooms

No Greek houses had hot and cold running water. Water for drinking, cooking, or washing had to be collected, in large jars called *hydrias,* from courtyard wells, springs, or fountains. Then, if necessary, water was heated over a flame. In hot, dusty ancient Greece, it was easy to get dirty, but very few homes would have had special rooms set aside for bathing. Some, however, were discovered during the **excavations** at Olynthos.

These were part of three-room blocks that each consisted of a large living room, a small bathroom, and a **flue,** separated off at one end by a partition. This partition may have been open at the top, to let heat and smoke pass through. The flue may also have served as a kind of dump for domestic trash, since so much broken pottery was found there.

Clues from painted pottery

At other sites, it is harder to tell where people washed, unless fragments of **terra-cotta** tubs are found in a certain place or spaces for tubs are found in the cement. **Archaeologists** do sometimes find pottery vessels with "bathroom scenes" painted on them, and we now know that, in some cases, the Greeks decorated their pots with pictures of the activity for which they were then used. So, if a vessel that shows people washing is found, there is a chance that the spot where it is found was once an ancient Greek bathroom.

This image from a *hydria* shows a woman washing her hair at a basin that stands on a pedestal.

What do the bathroom scenes show? Sometimes there are women washing at a large basin called a *louterion*, which had a **pedestal.** There might be vessels nearby, called *amphorae*, that were used for bringing water. Other scenes showed men washing in large basins, or scraping dead skin and dirt off their bodies with hand tools called *strigils*.

This is a terra-cotta model of a woman taking a bath, from the 5th century B.C.E.

Home hygiene

In his play *Wasps*, Aristophanes describes Philokleon coming home after he has served on a jury. He is greeted by his daughter, who praises him to get him to give her the money he has just earned:

"Oh then what a welcome I get for its sake;
my daughter is foremost of all,
and she washes my feet and anoints them with care
and above them she stoops and lets a kiss fall
till at last by means of her pretty 'Papas'
she angles my three **obols** pay."

Worship at Home

"There is never equality between the race of deathless gods and that of men who walk the Earth." Homer wrote this, and most of the ancient Greeks believed it. The Greeks saw things in opposites, and **deities** and mortals were just another example of this. Pindar wrote that, although both races sprang from Mother Earth, they were "kept apart by a difference in everything." In a long-ago "Golden Age," the Greeks believed, mortals and gods had dined together. Then, at the time of the first-ever sacrifice, the races were "divided." Every sacrifice after that time was a reminder of how wretched humankind was and how blessed the **immortals** were. Human beings could now make their offerings to the gods only from a very great distance.

Household religion

At large religious festivals, **citizen-priests** made sacrifices, hoping to win the favor and support of the gods and goddesses. There was no organized church with its own special officials, so when people wanted to worship in smaller groups, the most senior person present had to take charge. According to the **philosopher** Plato, all wise men were supposed to pray every morning and night, and the natural place to do this was in the home. Altars were set up in the courtyards of private homes. Then, the whole household worshiped together, with the head of the family supervising. While the public

This woman may be about to pour an offering at an altar to a god. The god himself may be the male figure pictured here.

The Greek family shown in this carving is worshiping together.

festivals honored the deities who were worshiped all over the Greek world, individual households prayed to more local gods and goddesses. Households also prayed to Zeus in his role as the defender of all family property, or "Zeus in the courtyard." A family's father might also make sacrifices and might seek blessings on behalf of the whole household. Families might even go on small religious processions.

Greek religion had more to do with rituals than with inner **spirituality.** It focused on group activity, not on a person's private faith. However, each household, with its little statue of the god Hermes standing outside, felt that its survival and success depended on a good relationship with the gods.

The family on Olympus

The ancient Greeks believed Zeus was the father figure of the household made up of the greatest Greek gods and goddesses who lived on the summit of Mount Olympus. Each of them was worshiped for particular purposes: Demeter for abundant crops, Pan for healthy flocks, Prometheus to watch over potters, and so on. When priests or heads of the household made gifts to these gods through sacrifices, they prayed for special favors in return, with words such as these:

"If ever I burned the rich thighs of bulls and goats in your honor, grant me this prayer."

Children in the Home

"Plainly we look to wives who will produce the best children for us and marry them to raise a family," wrote Xenophon. "The husband supports the wife who is to share in the production of his family, and provides in advance whatever he thinks the expected children will find useful in life." When a baby boy was born into a Greek family, a crown of olive leaves was pinned to the front door of the house. This was a symbol of success, even "victory." When a girl was born, her family pinned some wool to the door. This symbolized the domestic work that she would do for the rest of her life.

It seems that few children, if any, had their own rooms in Greek houses. As infants, they might have lived in the women's quarters and might have come to the more public rooms for special occasions. At times, they may have played in the courtyard, and they certainly took part in family prayers there. We know what kinds of toys they played with from the paintings on vases and also from "grave goods." These were items, such as clay dolls, puppets, tops, and rattles, that families buried with boys and girls who died young.

This **terra-cotta** doll with jointed limbs is an ancient Greek toy that has survived.

Short childhoods

Poorer children had to help run the household from a very early age. In richer families, boys might go to school from the age of seven, while girls stayed home to learn practical skills. At around the age of thirteen, girls were considered to be women. At a special ceremony, they dedicated their toys to the goddess Artemis, before putting them away forever. To show that they were grown-up, they wore a girdle around their waists. When they got married, perhaps as soon as two years later, they dedicated this girdle to Artemis, too.

Some children's toys have changed remarkably little since ancient times. The boy here is shown with a hoop. The man is holding a ball.

Greek Gardens?

◄► ◄► ◄► ◄► ◄► ◄► ◄► ◄► ◄► ◄► ◄► ◄► ◄► ◄► ◄► ◄► ◄► ◄► ◄►

The picture below shows the plan of a house that was built, in the 4th century B.C.E., at Eretria. This house was lived in for about 100 years. It covered the large area of about 2,250 square feet (about 625 square meters), but probably had only one single story.

Archaeologists have called it the House of the **Mosaics,** since so many of the floors were decorated. This suggests that the owners were rich people. It is fascinating to take a look at this home, room by room, and to try to imagine what might have happened in each of the inside spaces. As you will see, it may lead us to identify an unusual domestic space in ancient times—a garden.

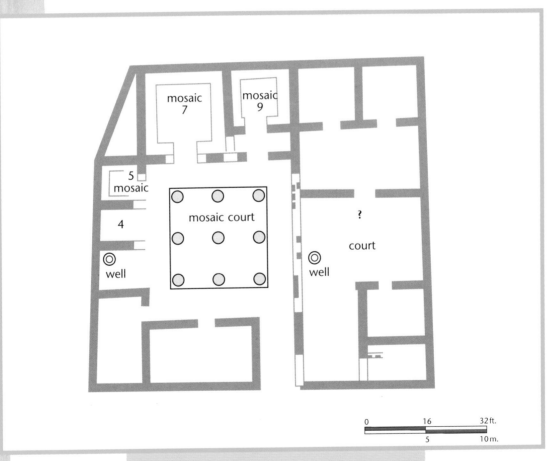

This is the archaeological plan of the House of Mosaics at Eretria, with its rooms numbered. Was the area marked "**?**" a rare ancient Greek garden?

A guided tour

People entered the house from the south and could go straight down a corridor into a central courtyard. Rooms 7 and 9 had raised benches for couches, so these were almost certainly the men's quarters. Room 5 may also have been an *andron*, while the small room next to it (room 4) could have been a cloakroom for guests. A marble table stood here, and there was a space for a large pottery vessel, which might have been a **chamber pot.** The neighboring room had a well in it, so that may have been for washing hands.

Hellenistic gardens

In Hellenistic times, the rich became more interested in **conspicuous consumption** than they had been in the Classical Age. Palm trees were imported into Greece, and a letter survives from an official in Alexandria who ordered his agent to plant 300 fir trees in the park on his **estate,** not only to supply timber for building ships but also for the trees' "striking appearance." Ordinary people also admired trees and flowers.

A long wall separated the western and eastern sections of the house. There must once have been a door in this wall. Rooms in the eastern part were arranged around a second open area, which also included a water supply. This open area showed few signs of having been paved over as the western courtyard had been. This led the archaeologists to deduce that it might have been a garden. If so, then it was an unusual feature in an ancient Greek home, at least before **Hellenistic** times.

Most houses, especially those in the cities, would not have been big enough to include a second courtyard. Most people, especially the poor, would not have had the time to cultivate a decorative garden. They relied on the plants grown in market gardens for their food.

How Do We Know?

The landscape of Greece is still littered with ruins from ancient times. Along with surviving Greek art and the work of Greek writers, this archaeological evidence often helps historians to form a clearer picture of the past. On page 16, you read about the important **excavations** that were made at Olynthos on the Chalkidiki peninsula. When the findings were published, in 1940, one of the **archaeologists** claimed that it would become "the main source of our evidence for the study of the Greek house."

Secrets revealed by the site

A large number of homes could be studied at Olynthos. From this, archaeologists discovered that there were a wide variety of houses in the city. Some of the dwellings were built to standard patterns, but it appeared that many had individual features, and were built to different **specifications.**

Olynthos looks like this today. Since no one has lived here since 348 B.C.E., it has been relatively easy for archaeologists to excavate this ancient site.

There was no direct evidence that the houses were divided into male and female areas. However, in light of ancient writings, the layouts do seem to suggest it. They also suggest that some members of the household—probably the women—were kept secluded from visitors. This can be deduced on the basis of the observation that there was only one door to each home. Access could therefore be controlled. When outsiders entered, their movement inside could be channeled, so that at least some part of the house remained out of bounds.

Yet no single site can ever tell the whole story. The findings at Olynthos must be set alongside discoveries that have been made at many other sites. You have read about some of these in this book. Together, they reveal a number of secrets about domestic life in ancient Greece. There is still so much that we do not know about Greek homes—especially the homes of the poor—and about how people lived in them. As you can see, there is still a great deal for archaeologists to find out.

Why *don't* we know?

Sparta was one of the greatest Greek city-states. Yet we must rely on written evidence for most of our information about it. Even in the 5th century B.C.E., Thucydides, who wrote eight thrilling books about the **Peloponnesian** War, foresaw how little other evidence the Spartans would leave behind. He wrote, "If the city of the Spartans were to become deserted and only the temples or the foundations of the buildings were left, I think that as time went by there would be few who would believe in Sparta's reputation—and yet it directly controls two-fifths of the Peloponnese, and dominates the rest and many cities outside it. It is not a coordinated city and has not got elaborate temples and buildings, but is formed of villages in the old Greek manner and would seem too insignificant."

Timeline

All the following dates are B.C.E.:

c. 3000–c. 1450	Greece is controlled by Minoan kings from Crete.
c. 1600–c. 1100	Greek-speaking Mycenaeans rule separate kingdoms in mainland Greece.
c. 1100–c. 800	Greece goes through a period of wars and migration.
c. 800–c. 700	Homer's *Iliad* and *Odyssey* were probably written; Greece is made up of small city-states that are ruled by separate kings or noble families
c. 750–c. 550	Greeks set up colonies in lands around the Mediterranean Sea.
c. 500	Some city-states become democracies; of these, Athens is the most powerful.
c. 490–479	The main period of **Persian** invasions of Greece occurs.
431–404	The **Peloponnesian** War, between Greek city-states, ends with Sparta eclipsing Athens as the most powerful state in mainland Greece.
378–371	Sparta is eclipsed by a new power, Thebes.
336–323	Greece is ruled by Alexander the Great of Macedon after his invasion and conquest.
146	Greece becomes part of the Roman Empire.

More Books to Read

Barron's Educational Editors. *Greek Life*. Hauppage, N.Y.: Barron's Educational Services, Inc., 1998.

Bartole, Mira, and Christine Ronan. *Ancient Greece*. Parsippany, N.J.: Pearson Learning, 1995.

Clare, John D., ed., *Ancient Greece*. New York: Harcourt Children's Books, 1994.

Day, Nancy. *Your Travel Guide to Ancient Greece*. Minneapolis: Lerner Publishing Group, 2000. An older reader can help you with this book.

Ganeri, Anita. *Ancient Greeks*. Danbury, Conn.: Franklin Watts, 1993.

Malam, John. *A Greek Town*. Danbury, Conn.: Franklin Watts, 1999.

Nardo, Don. *Life in Ancient Greece*. Farmington Hills, Mich.: The Gale Group, 1996. An older reader can help you with this book.

Pearson, Anne. *Ancient Greece*. New York: Dorling-Kindersley Publishers, Inc., 2000.

Rees, Rosemary. *The Ancient Greeks*. Chicago: Heinemann Library, 1997.

Glossary

archaeologist person who studies buildings and objects from the past to discover how people lived

barbarian anyone who was not Greek

barracks building or buildings in which soldiers live apart from other people

brazier metal container that holds lighted coals

chamber pot container used as a toilet

citizen person with the right to take part in politics, in particular, by voting

civilization distinct way of life that is common to a particular group of people

colonnade linked series of columns

conspicuous consumption spending of money on goods not necessary for survival

consumer durable product that does not wear out or get used up at once

deity god or goddess

disposing arranging

dowry marriage gift from the bride's family, usually consisting of money, land, or goods

drachma (more than one are called *drachmas*) silver coin that was the main Greek unit of money, worth six *obols*

economic made for financial reasons

estate all the property of a person, usually wealthy

excavate to dig up to be examined by archaeologists

flue channel or passage, often for transmission of heat

fresco painting made on a wall or ceiling before the plaster dries

heir person, usually a relative, who is given wealth or property from a person who has died

Hellenistic Greek influenced, or in the Greek style (from the Greek word *"Hellen,"* meaning a Greek)

immortal being that lives forever

inscription writing carved into a surface, such as a monument or a coin

lightsome full of light

lyre small, harplike musical instrument

menial low-level

metic foreigner, with some citizens' rights, living in a Greek city

mosaic design or picture made up of small pieces of colored stone, glass, or clay

obol small Greek silver coin. There were six *obols* to a *drachma*.

party walls walls shared by neighbors

pedestal base supporting a column, pillar, or other object

Peloponnese southern region of mainland Greece. This region includes the city-state of Sparta

peristyle circular formation of columns around a temple or courtyard. This term may also be used to refer to the space that is enclosed by such a formation.

Persian person who lived in the ancient Middle Eastern kingdom of Persia, which is now known as Iran

philosopher person interested in thoughts and theories, from the Greek words meaning lover of knowledge

polis (more than one are called *poleis*) Greek city-state

portico roof supported by columns at regular intervals

quarters one's own building or area of a building

servile like a slave, overly respectful in an insincere manner

specification instruction

spirituality feelings of a holy kind

staple basic kind of foodstuff

status position in society

status symbol personal belonging that shows one's status

stucco plaster or cement used to coat the surfaces of walls

terra-cotta unglazed pottery, usually brownish red in color

urban relating to a town or a city (not to the countryside)

vault series of arches that supports a roof

ventilation system for letting air move about freely

Index